Mr. Brian R. Hulse
107 Victory (
Milford, CT 0

MW00711024

Life is good

a guided gratitude journal

Caroll McKanna Shreeve

WALKING STICK PRESS
Cincinnati, Ohio

Life Is Good: A Guided Gratitude Journal. Copyright © 2001 by Caroll McKanna Shreeve.
Manufactured in the United States of America. All rights reserved. No part of this book may be
reproduced in any form or by any electronic or mechanical means including information storage and
retrieval systems without permission in writing from the publisher, except by a reviewer, who may quote
brief passages in a review. Published by Walking Stick Press, an imprint of F&W Publications, Inc., 1507
Dana Avenue, Cincinnati, Ohio, 45207. (800) 289-0963. First edition.

Visit our Web site at www.writersdigest.com for information on more resources for writers.

To receive a weekly E-mail newsletter delivering tips and updates about writing and about Writer's
Digest products, send an E-mail with "Subscribe Newsletter" in the body of the message to:
newsletter request@writersdigest.com, or register directly at our Web site at www.writersdigest.com.

05 04 03 02 01   5 4 3 2 1

Library of Congress Cataloging in Publication Data

Shreeve, Caroll McKanna, 1942-
    Life is good : a guided gratitude journal / Caroll McKanna Shreeve.
        p. cm.
    ISBN 1-58297-076-9 (alk.paper)
    1. Self-perception–Problems, exercises, etc. 2. Self-acceptance–Problems, exercises, etc. 3. Diaries–
Authorship. I. Title.

BF697.5.S43 S48 2001
158.01--dc21   2001026511
                                                                          CIP

Edited by Jack Heffron and Kim Agricola
Cover design by Lisa Buchanan
Interior layout by Donna Cozatchy
Cover photography by © Corbisstockmarket/Norbert Schäfer
Production coordinated by Mark Griffin

Dedication

To the sacred, creative Self
in each of us!

Acknowledgments

With loving gratitude...

to thousands of student and client friends, to my children, Kimbra, Sean, Kimberly and Michelle, and my grandsons, Tarren and Isaac, to my poetry-loving father, Bob McKanna, and to my brother, Curt Hersey, who have all—over the years—shared their words and drawings with me, opened their hearts and minds, and awed me with their trust in the creative process.

To my photographer/filmmaker friend, Marion Duckworth Smith; to my poet friend, Theresa Pryor Kohl; to my sketchbook-journaling, play and teatime friend, Leslie Trottier; to my author/illustrator friend, Rose Offner; to my graphic design friend, Lezlie Reinking Sokolik; to my author friend and father of our two children, Dr. Richard Halley, who first pushed me to share my writing; to my author friend, DuAnne Nebeker, whose Spirit coaching delights me; and to my book group of talented and prolific writing and illustrating soul sisters, Lynn Champagne, Karen Foster, and Sally Lindsay.

To Jack Heffron, Kim Agricola, and other Writer's Digest editors, and to designers Clare Finney and Lisa Buchanan, all who have supported my concept for this book and helped me hone its beauty and usefulness.

All have believed in me and inspired me to dig into my soul's sand for fun and Self-discovery. I thank them for encouraging me to trust what I find there, helping me polish it and urging me to pass it on.

I love you all.

And not least to my dear husband, Brent Shreeve, my partner in life and business, and my safe and supportive haven, who affirms with me that to risk Self-discovery together is to learn over and over again that . . .

Life is truly, deeply, joyfully good!

An author advocate with her own writing and illustrating career, Caroll juggles a thirteen-year-old Utah publishing/consulting services business with teaching as an adjunct professor in English at Weber State University and book pre-press and marketing for the University of Utah's Life-long Learning program.

She has been a speaker for Reader's Digest Magazine Writing Workshops and Writer's Digest conferences, and a contributing editor to **Junction** magazine, for which she writes the monthly art-critic column, "Visually Speaking . . . ."

She is a reviewer of college English textbooks for Prentice Hall and writes for children under the pen name and childhood moniker of Susie McGruder McGlish. Caroll has taught fine arts in public and private schools in Ohio, Maine, New Hampshire, Virginia, and Utah at all levels from primary and secondary through university.

She is the former vice president of publishing and editor in chief of Meridian International, a custom-magazine house where she contributed more than 250 articles to their ten monthly magazines and headed a team of editors in genres from bridal and business to sports, health and travel.

As an in-house editor of garden, art, spiritual self-help, and cookbooks for Gibbs Smith Publisher, Peregrine Smith Books, Utah, she fell further in love with her consulting support business helping authors and illustrators prepare their book ideas for publishers.

Her first novel, **Farr Trials**, took a prize in the Utah Arts Council 2000 fiction competition and is with her agent.

Caroll is the wife of Brent "Art" Shreeve. Between them, they share four children and two grandchildren.

table of
Contents

Materials List

Writing Pens	Fine, broad line, or calligraphy pens Gel pens in various colors like pastels or metallic gold, silver, or copper
Art Supplies	Lead sketching pencils in various shades Watercolors/brushes Colored pencils (clay or wax-bound) Markers (beware of bleed-through) Coffee, tea, beet juice, chalk, and fixative
Craft Supplies	Colored paper Gift wrap Wallpaper scraps Magazine cutouts Stickers Rubber stamps Glitter, ribbon, string, yarn, and foil Buttons and beads Photographs
Nature Materials	Pressed flower blossoms and leaves Grass, seeds, feathers, and stones Tea leaves, coffee grounds, and fine-grain sand
Other Tools	Liquid glue/glue stick Scissors (decorative-edged and straight-cut) Hole punch Mounting-spray glue

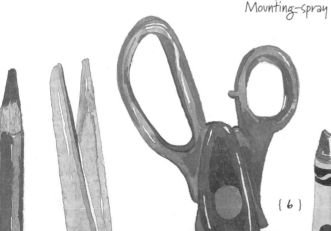

How to Use This

journal

Perhaps like me, your soul's language has been writing and drawing since both were nothing but scribbles to anyone but ourselves. This guided journal offers thirty-one awakening activities designed for purposeful play and adventurous Self-discovery. Think of this book as your virtual sandbox.

Why a guided journal?

When we were children, everything became a tool for fun. We no't only scribbled with crayons and pencils, but with sticks in the dirt and ketchup on the trays of our high chairs. We arranged stones, buttons, and leaves in patterns we found pleasing, just because we liked them our certain way.

We wrote in circles and upside down. We spelled words backward and in code. We stopped and started sentences any place we felt like, it It's time to return to that blissful state of mind, particularly if it's been a long

time since you felt in complete control of anything in your life. Nothing heals hurts, restores confidence, and nourishes life with joy like creating your own journal pages.

We are all artists and writers at heart. Forget skill levels and target for joy.

If you think writing and drawing are scary at first, that is sign number one that you need to honor your spirit with a safe place to play. Let your journal become your sandbox. Color or cover over my sketches and add your own art. Have fun! There are no lines you have to stay inside.

Retreat here as often as you can, even if it's only for a few minutes at a time. Write a note or a quote that you find meaningful. Paste in a beautiful leaf from a morning walk or the corner of a napkin you wrote on over coffee. Come back to them another day. What do they mean to you? Why were they special? Ask and answer your own questions directly on the pages. Your answers will often surprise and delight you.

Get to know your Self. If you're like most people, you take care of everyone else all the time. It's your turn. Your soul is hungry for meaning to be found inside and all around you. Get in touch with your connection to your spirit Self and our precious universe.

This is not a diary with demanding dates that beg for sequence and moving on to the next page. You can return to the same page as many times as you want—days, weeks, or months after you begin.

Your sandbox journal can become your survivor's manual. Color, embellish, or cover over any of the sketches you want. You can doodle through a nearly unbearable meeting and appear—to the speaker—to be taking copious and important notes. Who knows, some kernel of significance to your passage may be a gift of your speaker or someone whom you sit near. One of my students has a journal reserved for special times when he gives himself a "mental health" day; another has a Friday Fun Book. For others, their

journals are where they "dig" into their hurts, sort them like buttons, and bury them in the sand, literally gluing sand all over the private pains they want "never to dig up again."

Gluing ribbons, tabs, stickers, and other helpful markers for returning with ease to special "epiphany" pages is another way to personalize your journal. Glue in beautifully decorated or plain and practical envelopes for notes and tidbits. Where do you begin? Why not at the back or in the middle of your journal for a change? Who says you have to start at the front of every book to begin?

What writing and art supplies are best to use in journaling?

Consider any material an art tool if you use it to write or draw, if you paste it into your journal, or if it pleases you. If you don't draw, you can cut pictures from magazines. Download images off the Net, print, and then cut them out and spray-mount or glue them to the pages. Paint with cold tea and coffee, beet juice and lemon. (Well, lemon disappears. Remember secret messages?) If you write backward it can only be read in a mirror. If you want to get fancy, there are art and craft materials galore that range in cost from pennies to as many dollars as you want to spend.

If you do buy something special, consider a silver metallic pen for secrets because they are difficult to read at a glance—if anyone snoops over your shoulder—and the silver words and lines look so sacred and sophisticated that you'll feel like an author and illustrator immediately. Gold, copper, and your favorite colors will provide you the beauty that artist/calligrapher monks in ages past knew when illuminating precious manuscripts with fancy letters, flowers, and figures. Your words and images are just as precious and just as worthy of an honored book.

When we draw we really see. When we describe our world we really write. When we feel and describe in word and picture images, we learn who we are. You can't forgive and love someone well whom you don't even know.

Here in your journal "sandbox," your safe place, you can find out that it's safe to grow up. You can take better care of your Self by learning about you and setting boundaries that others learn to respect. If you've already discovered that truism, you know that life is good! Keeping it that way means staying in your process of celebrating and growing. Journaling is a healthy adventure you deserve.

Know your Self; love your Self; forgive your Self; heal your Self; free your Self; celebrate your Self!

Awaken to the goodness of you.

Celebrate in these pages that life is good!

PART 1

Awaken to

creativity

Discover the Sacred in

the Ordinary

Simple

pleasures

Are you having trouble feeling comfortable with a clean page? Afraid to "mess up" your new book? Make friends with your writer and illustrator tools. Devote a few pages to writing and drawing in lines, dots, squiggles, shapes, flowers, balls, umbrellas, shovels, pails, squares, triangles, or any patterns that you can make with pen, pencil, brush, crayon, color marker, white correction fluid marker, stamp shape, or other tool to begin the fun of making this book uniquely yours.

Fill the pages.

Study what you made.

Turn the book upside down.

Add something.

Relax. You've just created practice patterns. Borrow from them when you want to make a special design on other pages.

Trust your Self.

When you were a kid you knew this was art.

Remember and enjoy.

My tools and I
make my art.
My way of
creating is
sacred to me
and to my
Maker.

Looking for the Sacred

in the ordinary

Now that you are soul-deep in your sandbox journal, it's time to have fun!

Journal in hand, take a walk around wherever you are, indoors or outside.

Really notice your image in the most unusual places, as if you were in the fun house at an amusement park.

Draw and write about the joys of finding your tiny Self on a shiny tea kettle, a faucet, or a doorknob; reflected in someone else's glasses or eyes, in the rearview mirror, or on the bumper of your car; stretched long and skinny in a picture frame;

made round and fat on the toe of a shiny shoe; and looking back at your Self from a shop window.

All of the wonderful images are you. Realize that your importance to others is everywhere, whether you are conscious of it or not.

You are mysteriously clear or outrageously distorted according to the eye of the beholder.

Inside where it counts, you are always you.

Smile with the pleasure of your own mystery, and laugh at the fun of finding your Self in fresh ways.

Inside where

it counts,

I am

always me.

A Cup of

steaming soul

Prepare a hot cup of your favorite beverage: tea, coffee, cocoa, water with lemon, cider with cinnamon—any drink you like!

As you sip, experience the steam, the aroma, the flavor, the color of the liquid, the warmth of the cup, even the memories of other moments with such a steaming cup. Write about your musings. Stay in the moment. The moment is one of the soul's blessings.

Leave a tablespoon or two of dregs in the cup.

With a brush, a cotton swab, a toothpick, or a feather quill, dip into the cup and paint shapes using the liquid you have been drinking.

Realize that life is art.

Everything in our world is a tool for beauty and a connection to ourselves and all the elements of the universe.

Life is good, especially in its most ordinary moments.

My moments
are precious,
for my senses
keep me in
touch with
my Self and
our world.

Life is art.

I am alive.

I am artful, too.

Starting from

scrap

Go to a trash bin or a wastebasket and select an interesting scrap. Glue it into your journal. By drawing or painting, cutting or pasting, make the scrap into an animal with the necessary ears, legs, tail, horns, wings, or whatever. Name your animal some whimsical title that is appropriate to what it is and where it came from. Make pictures and write about animals of importance in your life. What gifts did they bring? What gifts did you share?

Next time you're in the library or on the Internet, look up in a tarot book or a Chinese or native folklore source the symbolic nature of the animal you made. How is it a totem for your power in certain lifeways? Write about the clues to you.

As a follow-up activity, use paper scraps to make a bridge and write about how you are or can be connected to good books, good tools, good people, good music, and a good life.

Write about what you can do to link your Self to what you value, with a chain of friends and experiences to make good happen.

Drawing

your self

Standing in this sandbox, consider that we are more than the obstacles we have survived. On my birthdays I used to sit before a mirror and draw or paint a portrait of my Self. I made it a practice to always write a response to the "who" in the mirror. When I responded to my Self with "Learning to relax with black in the background," I recognized a spiritual growth spurt. The pose, the smile, the colors, and the nuances expressed a new comfort level I had reached in my own skin. I had learned to forgive, even my Self, and to love even me. It was a moment of awakening to freedom. It was a gift only I could give my Self.

Draw or paint your mirror image—perhaps just a portion of your Self—or make a portrait of a favorite shoe, or trace your foot.

Write about who you are on your path right now, the obstacles you have left behind, the rivers of experience you would love to dip a toe into, the mysteries of the path ahead, the daily down-payment steps you are taking to be true to your own goal destinations—even and especially when it's hard, or when no one else honors your dream.

Honor you.

I am not the
path I have
trod. I am
more than my
overcomings,
more than my
achievements.

I am me.

I give my
Self the gift
of stepping
into my dream
on my own
soul's path.

purpose

There is a part of you that seeks to awaken! Each of us
has a purpose within and beyond the moment. We bring
into our lives what we desire at some level to work on,
to build, to improve, to let go of. Sometimes it seems
trivial or scary to open our eyes to our inner mysteries.
Why are we drawn to a beautiful person, object,
handcraft, bird, or flower? Write about the bud that
wishes to burst into blossom in your life.

Begin in a spiral to write out a stream of sleeping
thoughts about the people in your life whom you have
drawn close to (or would like to) because they reflect to
your soul some dream you would like to manifest in your
own life.

Commit in writing to a first step, however tiny it is.

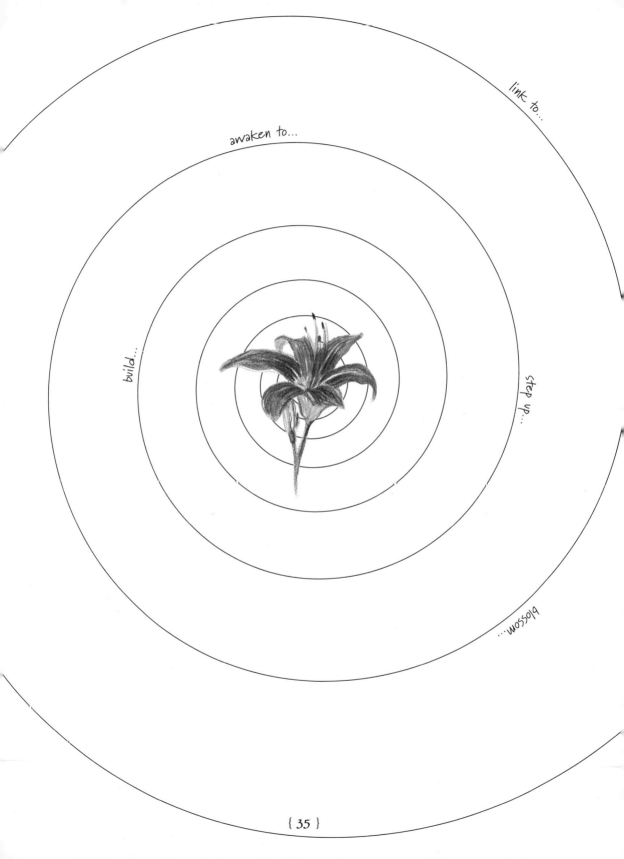

link to...

awaken to...

build...

step up...

blossom...

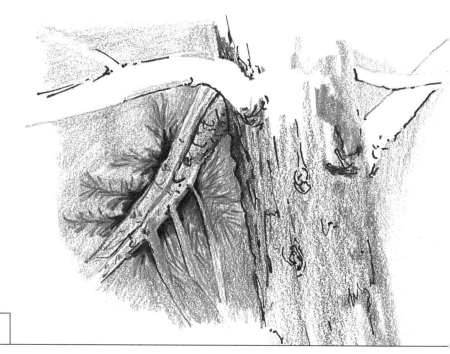

PART 2

Awaken to

nature

Celebrate Its Energy

and Wonder

Living Details

Using nature materials and glue, paint or drawing tools, create pleasing patterns on your journal page that are your own "made up" nature arrangements. Write to your Self about you as a creator taking found materials to make something new and worthwhile.

Realize in your words how sacred the creative process is: the selection of materials, the arrangement of parts, the making of beauty, and the joy in the making. Bless this gift of creative power that is shared with us from God, the universe, or Spirit—whatever your name for the force for "making" that is greater than we are. Honor it with your own creativity.

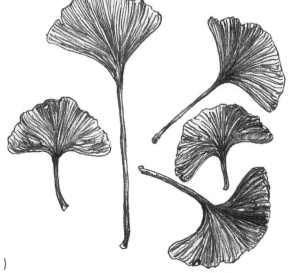

faith

Take a stroll around your home or
neighborhood and uproot a weed; tiny is fine.
Shake off the dirt and examine its delicate roots.
Draw them the best you can. Honor them. Think of all the
work they do. They explore every crevice of earth available
to find sustenance to add to water and sunlight in the growth
process of that plant. The leaves above ground absorb sunlight
without questioning if the roots below are doing their part.

Write about your roots. What do you value? What and who do
you count on to nourish and sustain you? If your roots need
better ground for more nourishment, write about what you can
do to feed your Self. Remember that you are rooted to your
Maker through the creative process. Act in faith that you
have purpose, and send out your own new shoots for good.

Geometry in

nature

Take a nature observation walk, even if it's only inside your home studying your houseplants or your goldfish. Draw and write about the forms and patterns of nature that you see. Write that you are part of the Big Plan. You were not unwanted by life; you were not an accident; you have a purpose.

Your purpose is as big as the plan itself. Write about how you embrace your part in the good, not just for others—for you!

Discover where you are blooming in the infinite pattern of the universe.

You embody:

spent flowers,

opening

blossoms, tiny

buds of the

ever-new you.

I am a
necessary part
of the
Big Plan,
an ever-new
detail in the
universal
geometry.
No one else
can fulfill my
role here.

Beginnings *and endings*

Select an egg, a seed, a seashell, a bud, a burned tree, a fallen bird, or blossom — some evidence of the beginning or ending of life as we know it. Draw it carefully.

Write about the beginnings and endings in your life, what they have meant and why they matter, especially to you. Give thanks for beginnings and for endings. Both are evidence of life's—and your own—continuing journey.

In the circle
of life,
endings and
beginnings are
necessary
passages and
transformations.

Sometimes it
is required
that I find a
new way to
bloom where
I am, or end
what does
not work in
my life.

Whichever I
choose, it is
always a
new beginning
that will
ripple with
consequences.

stone

When we plunk a stone into an expanse of water, we watch as the circling ripples send the news in every direction. It takes a long time for the circles to dissipate. (The next time you take a bath, plunk in your bar of soap and watch the news travel to your toes again and again.)

Our lives are like that.

Draw or glue cut-paper stones, then write about the hard stones that have been dropped into your life. Write about the funny stones that have sent ripples of laughter into your days, and the holy stones of love and tenderness that have circled you with sweet meaning or safety.

All are important, just as you are.

Save one stone to represent your Self. Label it with your name. Don't worry if your stone is rough or worn, polished or new. You are important in the sands of time. Your business here is bottom-line valuable.

Write about the hard and beautiful ways you have plunked into the lives of others. Thank those who recognized your visit for good. Forgive those who weren't watching their toes. Write a forgiving message to your Self if you startled the unsuspecting with your stone—you did what you understood at the time. Next time, think like water and go to the low places with your soothing love. Consider soothing your Self, too.

I am a stone
of goodness.
I can choose
where, when,
and how I will
plunk my love
and send it
circling into
the lives
of others.

My circle of
love goes
beyond my
view. I send
ripples inside
my Self, too.

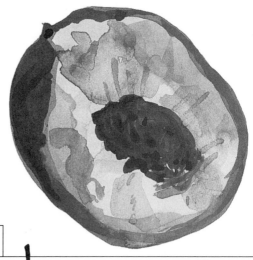

Share Your Journey and Plant

seeds for good

Gather seeds. Notice the dried peppercorns, coffee and vanilla beans, lentils, soup beans, sesame seeds, fresh apple, pear, grape, sweet, or chile pepper seeds. Do you see how each is unique? We are each unique little miracles in the scheme of growing, too. No one else has our voice, our fingerprints, our eye/pupil configuration, our DNA. Draw some seed portraits.

Write about you as a seed for good to your Self. (We are always planting for others.) What seeds of love and comfort can you plant and nourish within your own heart, mind, and body?

Seeds of
kindness must
sprout first
in your
heart before
you plant
elsewhere.

PART 3

Awaken to

spirit

Connect to

Its Good Purpose

in Your Life

Containers of

purpose

Select a glass container that can hold air, water, buttons, stones, marbles, beans, sugar, etc. Fill it as far as you want to and then draw or paint your interpretation of this purposeful container full of important "stuff." Even invisible air is "in there." We couldn't live without it, so don't discount its importance. Did you sort buttons or marbles as a child? Write about your memories of important containers you recall.

Some people believe our souls surround our bodies. Others think our bodies "hold" our souls. You "contain" your heart.

Glue in an envelope that fits this journal. Make it beautiful with your designs.

Write a letter to your Self about all the mysterious and wonderful things you hold inside. Fold it and place it for safe-keeping in your envelope. Reread your letter regularly. Add to it as you realize more good "stuff" about your Self.

A Container of My Purpose!

Close the flap with a removable sticker so you can get into your envelope as often as you like.

spirit

words

In this space, using your nondominant hand, write spirit words that represent good ideas and stories you hold inside that you'd like to let out into your sandbox and play with.

Write about the
consequences
you imagine
that would
possibly occur
for good or
difficulty if
the good
purposes you
hold inside
your "heart"
container
were allowed
to work in
your life.
(Only you can
define what
"good" means
for a private
purpose you
wish to
manifest in
your life.)

Handles and

Select an item that has one or more handles from your kitchen, garage, basement, or closet. Pose it pleasantly; draw or paint it with friendly art materials on your journal pages. Enjoy the process of creating line, form, color, dark, and light. Let your Self lose track of time.

Look at your Self in a full-length mirror. Place your hands on your hips like a sugar bowl. Write about all of the things that you "handle" for others in your life. Write about what others "handle" for you. Think about what is inside and outside your "handling" control.

Vow to let go of what is outside your handling capacity. Look in that mirror again. Release your elbow handles and embrace your Self. That's right, give your Self a hug.

Write about who hugs you or who doesn't, and how it feels. Ask your Self who would appreciate a hug from you.

Consider if you feel safe and wise enough to give it.

The Body Tells Us Our

truth

Embrace your Self's physical
discomfort as a messenger of
change for good that needs
to happen. Write about where
you ache or don't function
well in your body. Pick a
part of your body and
draw it with great care.

Write to that body part and
thank it for its service to
you and others. Vow to take
better care of your body.
Begin by loving all of your
physical parts. Listen to them.

When my
foot hurts,
do I fear
a life step?
When my
heart aches,
is there
a painful
relationship? Is
the pain with
my Self?

When my
elbow hurts,
am I bending
it toward my
mouth more
often than
my body needs
food fuel?

When my
shoulders or
back hurt,
do I carry
the burdens
of others?
Am I crippling
or helping
them?

Cracks and

wrinkles

Find evidence of cracking, peeling, wrinkling, or torn wear on an item that you have in your environment or within your regular view. Perhaps it is a well-loved object, perhaps it's hardly noticed.

Draw or paint it into your journal. (A photo is okay, too.)

Write about its history of giving and the meaning of its use.

Think and write about your own wrinkles, scars, and evidences of wear and worth. Our histories are evident. Celebrate your worth and do not despair that inside and outside our choices are apparent to others. Are you happy with those choices and their appearance? It is never too late to accept our wear and to approve what we have in our hearts, our minds, and our bodies.

My inner
worth is more
than my outer
appearance.

I celebrate
my Self, my
heartbreaks,
and my scars.

Color's Role in

self Language

For most of us, when we were small our favorite colors changed as we discovered new reasons for liking colors. We do have color preferences for everything from our cars and home interiors to our hair and clothing.

Colors relate to different meanings in each culture. What matters is what colors you prefer, even if your favorites are secret! It's amazing how many people don't wear or live with the colors they really like the most! If this is true for you, write about why.

With your art materials, color or cut and paste colorful shapes, designs, and patterns onto these pages.

Write about your favorite colors and the reasons why they matter to you. Note in descriptive terms how these colors, visual textures, or designs have meaning and spiritual story power for you. Decorate these pages; in fact, decorate your entire journal! It's you!

Color of sun,

color of water,

color of blood,

color of fire,

color of snow,

color of skin,

color of joy,

color of sadness,

color of hope.

All are full of power.

Building Creates Our

Link to spirit

The act of building something requires our creative Self. Remember that creativity is our spirit's sacred process link to our Maker, creator, God.

In the same way, your most clever, creative, and resourceful Self can connect you to good people, good books, good music, good health, good jobs—whatever your life needs to experience.

Build a boat for a puddle or for your bathtub. Use toothpicks, twigs, can lids, plastic bags, a bar of soap, or whatever materials occur to your bright mind. Sail it! Write about where it will take your imagination! Describe your destination in words.

Create a literal bridge that can stand up on your bureau or a favored shelf. Think about what it can connect in your life. Go from wish to good, or good to good, or from hurt to healing.

Write about how you are a "good" builder active in the construction—not destruction—business. Make good happen.

PART 4

Awaken to

story

Explore Its Symbolic

Meaning for You

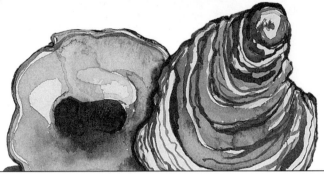

from grit

Pearls don't just appear by magic, they grow from grit. Sometimes an irritating Self characteristic, other person, or outside event bugs us enough that we focus on making it a smooth, beautiful "gem" in our lives.

Fold a sheet of stiff paper in half lengthwise (the stiff card paper in a shirt box or pantyhose package is perfect). Using the fold as a hinge, cut out three oyster shells (or any other shell form that you like). Glue the bottom half of each to the following pages so that they have a top shell flap. Decorate your shells so they are beautiful. They represent you.

Lift the top shell of each so you can glue in a bead, button, fake pearl, sequin, half of a lentil bean, or anything pleasing that can represent a "pearl."

Near each shell, write about a piece of grit in your life that has already or could in the future become a pearl that is meaningful, beautiful, and a true treasure. If all of your pearls are outside your Self, vow to make a pearl of some personal grit that you can layer with enough Self-love to ease its irritation.

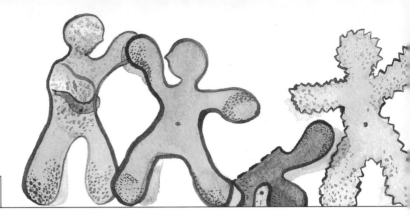

Embracing Our

sandpaper people

There are always people in our lives whom we allow to absorb our attention, our energy, and our concern or anger. Realize that we bring into our lives the relationships that we require to reflect something that we admire or disdain in our Selves. Think about those specific people in your life. (They may even be dead.)

Using sandpaper scraps or glue and fine-grain sand, dried tea leaves, or coffee grounds, create at least one shape on a journal page that represents that person. Write about the person's strengths and shortcomings. Explore how the person reflects what you like most and least about your Self. Embrace that sandpaper person in your life with gratitude. Vow to celebrate the person's goodness and to use his or her lacks as a life lesson.

When I
accept the
teaching gift
brought to
me by the
challenging
people in my
life, I learn
life lessons
about my Self
that free me
to live with
more integrity.

It feels good
to walk
my talk.

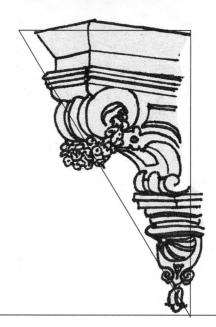

triangles

Architecturally speaking, the triangle is the most stable form in nature and in constructed bridges and buildings. It is the shape used to represent mountains and symbolic images of strength, creativity, and connection to the universal plan. Triangles of various shapes are found in leaves and tree forms.

Draw or cut out and glue in triangle shapes. Decorate each with nature images in patterns or in single designs that please you, or fill the shapes artfully with building or bridge elements.

Write about your creative Self and the stories of the stable evidences of your abilities to put things together in a pleasing way for your Self and others. Do you build, restore, cook, sew, craft, garden, dance, make music, solve problems?

I am a vital
part of the
sacred creative
process. What
I choose to
make has
value in the
symbolic and
holy act of
making, as
well as in the
results.

Stuffed and Inanimate

conversations

When we were children, we could play and imagine for
hours with stuffed animals, dolls, electric trains, blocks,
and all kinds of toys. Toys and imagination made us
happy. We talked to them and they to us. They were
our friends.

Find a toy or keepsake and draw or paint it. Ask it
questions about its experiences. Listen! Write down the
answers. Tell it how important your favorite toy was to
your child Self. Tell it how important it is to you. Write
about your toy stories.

Identify the ways you play today, and if you can't find
any, vow to make this journal your beginning. Your soul
needs a safe place to play.

Symbolic Self

stories

Select one opaque and one transparent object (plant life or person-made) and draw or paint both of them. Write about the secrets (energy? seeds? jewels?) they hold.

Write a symbolic story about how you have the power to reveal or keep secret what is in your best interests of safety and good. You can choose to be "see-through" or "secret." Selecting wisely feels good.

This peeling
narcissus bulb
is bursting
with a secret
of life,
flaming its
green into the
atmosphere
from a heart
pumping with
energy and
the need
to grow.

I want to be
like that;
don't you?

Just because
I don't tell
everyone my
secrets doesn't
mean I'm
not a good,
honest person.
Sometimes
it means I
am wise.

I have a right
to be safe as
well as good.

moments

Think of a beautiful moment in your childhood or teen years. It's okay if it was an ordinary place or time. Where were you? What was happening? Who were you with? Why do you recall the moment as special?

Write your answers to those questions and include a story about a favorite good moment in your childhood.

Write the name of a child you could bless in a similar way. It's okay if the child is now in grown-up skin. It's okay if the child is your Self!

Write about a place or person(s) that you would enjoy being with for a special moment in the future. Vow to give your Self permission to experience a good and right thing.

My life story
has meaning
that is
bigger and
more important
than I imagine.

My special
moments are
highlights of
my story. I am
more than my
low moments,
more than my
struggles.

PART 5

Awaken to

self-worth

The Beauty You Notice

Is About Who You Are

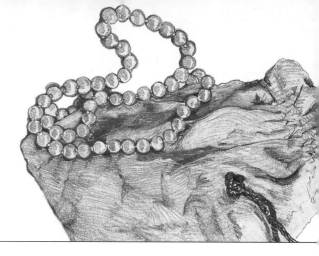

String of

pearls

There are significant people, animals, and events in our lives that we can think of symbolically as pearls on our life neckace.

Find a ribbon, a length of yarn, embroidery floss, or a piece of string. Tie several knots in it, then arrange it onto a journal page. Secure it with blobs of liquid glue at each knot. Allow the remaining string to be free or glue it down, as you choose. Allow the blob "pearls" to dry completely. (This requires hours, so leave your journal open to the air.)

Label each pearl with the name of a person, animal, or special event in the necklace of your life.

Write about each of the precious pearls you have linked. Write about the pearl you are to others.

Create another necklace.

Label a pearl with your name. Label each of the other pearls with the names of good books, good people, good animals, and good experiences that you link your own goodness to in this life.

Write about the importance of these good things to you. Think about how long it has been since you enjoyed the touch of each of these pearls.

If too many of them are in the past or await you in the future, get in touch with at least one of your pearls within twenty-four hours.

Living in the
now is full of
good. Self
needs to live
fully in the
moment.

I give up
putting off
being in touch
with good
each day.

I am a pearl
of great
price in
the Big Plan.

clean

Space for More Good

The older we get, the more we gather "stuff" in our lives and in our psyches. It's helpful to do an assessment and a bit of literal or mental housecleaning. It is important to "let go" in order to grow. It is healthy to clear out and erase the "no longer needed" in our lives and minds to make room for more good. (Sometimes negative people are on that list.)

With an erasable pencil, write about belongings, people, and "must do" responsibilities you could do without to make your life really good. When you finish, erase! See the room you've made for more good in your life? Vow to have the guts to do it.

The Feng-shui
awakening
is a deeply
meaningful
cleansing and
simplifying
process that is
life-enriching
at many levels.

Erase and
sweep away
debris. Be
free for
new good.

The Peanut Butter in

whose sandwich?

If we imagine ourselves as peanut butter sandwiched between others in our lives, the picture is clear that sometimes we get spread pretty thin. It's not always a healthy sandwich.

Cut out a pair of paper bread slices and glue one of them into your journal. With thick paint (a peanut butter brown or jelly color), paint words or shapes on the glued slice that represent your role in somebody else's sandwich: at home, on the job, in life.

While the paint dries, write about how it feels to be the peanut butter. Are you feeding or sticking to the roof of someone's mouth, choking off their ability to feed themselves?

When the goo is dry, paste the other paper slice on top. Are you trapped? Do you want to stay in there? What is good for you and your family? You have choices in sandwich making.

Do I need to
get out of
someone else's
way so they
can learn to
make their
own nutritious
sandwich?

Does anybody care that I'm the peanut butter holding them together?

What would happen if I stayed in my container?

Listening for

my good

One of the most rewarding ways to awaken to good in our Selves is to notice the myriad details in nature. An especially soul-soothing detail is good sound.

Turn off technology in your home or yard, or go for a hike. Pay attention selectively to nature sounds: wind in leaves or grasses, bird calls, animal noises, children laughing, thunder and lightning, insects buzzing, plops of rain, rushing streams, or roaring surf. With an attitude of gratitude, write about your sensory experience and how it enhanced your sense of Self.

Take a sound, touch, scent, or taste "sensory imagery tour" often. Invite a child along. Share the adventure of listening and smelling as our Native American and early-settler ancestors did. It's a good stress-relieving way to restore perspective on our world and our place in it. It has been said that God is in the details. In the cosmic Plan, we too are details, no less important.

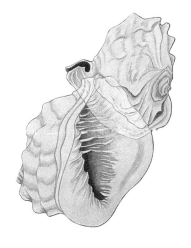

The sound of

a breeze

riffling

through palm

fronds and

leaves is

nature music.

My soul

understands it.

I am wise to
good music.
My soul hears
the most
delicate sounds
and is happy.

Celebrating

self-worth

Romance is a heart-worthy word, so rarely used for our Selves. Yet if we can't fall in love with our Selves, whom can we expect to wholeheartedly love us?

How long has it been since you danced, cut out paper hearts, wrote a love note or a poem, bought a long-stem rose, sang a song? Who says you have to save those experiences for other loved ones? Pick one and DO it! Write about your Self-romance experience.

Create good life heartbeat rhythms for your Self. It will give you so much more good to share with others. Refuel you! It's healthy for your heart and for your spirit.

My heart belongs to
me—first!

sing . . .

dance . . .

romance . . .

chance . . .

I cannot
expect others
to make my
heart sing. It
is up to me to
love my Self.

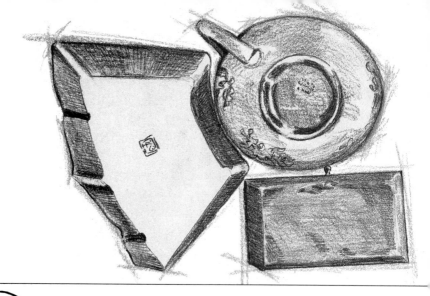

Soles of

good

Select three objects from your belongings with interesting bottom shapes. Arrange them close together—upside down. Draw or paint them (trace their bottoms if you prefer). Write about the shapes and how they are an important part of the role each object plays—for example, shoes or jewelry and where they have been.

Write about your little-noticed or appreciated aspects of Self. Imagine turning just one facet of you upside down or right-side out as a "what if" surprise. Write about what good new thing might happen in your life. How would you feel and behave? Why? Who would be impressed or shocked? Why?

It is a risk to
be true to
Self. It is a
risk to not be
true to Self.
Either way
there may be
uncomfortable
consequences.

I am the only
one who
knows what I
am willing to
risk to feel
comfy in my
own skin.

Genuine Gifts Are

good for you

Sometimes the hardest thing for us to do is to accept the compliments and gifts of others. We may fear attachments, "strings," obligations, or deceit. When you can discern that the givers and their purposes are genuine, teach your Self to accept a sign of your worth. Embrace the giver and the gift. Realize others need to give to feel good, too (just as you do).

Write about a time when someone gave you something that you treasure or that you had trouble freeing your Self to say "thank you" for, or that perhaps you didn't think you deserved. (You did deserve it and more.) In the least say, "Thank you for the thought."

Draw, paint, or glue in a photo "portrait" of a good gift from someone to you, even from your Self.

Write about its importance as a declaration of your worthiness to receive, as well as the giver's importance in recognizing your value.

A friend
asked me
what I'd really
enjoy as a
gift. She lives
where Queen
Anne's Lace
grows. I miss
it and told
her so.

She gathered
some blossoms,
pressed and
dried them,
tied them
with ribbon
and sent me
her gift from
nature and
her Self.

I was thrilled!

I told her so.

Write about
how it feels
to receive and
to give. Which
is the more
difficult for
you? Why?

Realize that
you are your
Maker's gift
to life and to
the universe.
You are
worthy just
because you
are worthy.

The Maker
"don't make
junk." Isn't it
good that life
is good?

It is good that

life is good!

Enjoy it . . . share it.